GENIUS THE
SORCERESS

ANAIYA SHAH

Table of Contents

Part 1

MOVIE MAGIC

Once upon a time, there was a land called MOVIE MAGIC. It was not very popular because not many people knew about it. If all knew about this magical land, it would be so very popular. It would have tourists streaming in and out of it. This land is at the very edge of the world. There aren't any legends for anybody to tell. It is quite a secret, so I trust you not to tell anyone either.

SSHHHhhhh!!!!!

So here I am, telling you secret and forbidden tales of MOVIE MAGIC. We are the true ones who make movies, not Dizzy + or whatever that is. And not that Net Flakes. Pause, wait, why am I even telling you these things? Oh, well.

So, here I'm going to tell you some of our biggest and darkest secrets: We often use potions. We also even use potions on people.

Wooohhffffff!!!!!!!!

There, our most secret, secret of all time. How do we accomplish this? Well, we disguise ourselves.

DUH!

You see, I didn't always know any of this was possible. My expectations for life were to someday become queen, and live a boring life in a castle that was probably thousands of years old. Here's my story about something important that has been happening in MOVIE MAGIC and how my story mostly began:

Hi, I'm Genius, the daughter of Queen Isha. So, whoops, spilled the tea; I'm a princess. Yeah, I hate being a princess. Not because of silly old paparazzi. (We don't have paparazzi to worry about, actually). I wish I had a normal life. I don't like to be bothered. So one day, I was just relaxing in the castle when my mom came in.

She said, "You are going to go to a school in Miikay." (Pronounced my-key).

"What!?" I exclaimed. "I refuse to go."

"You will go, Genius; go and pack your things. I expect to see you outside in thirty minutes."

"When am I going to see you again?" "In four months," said my mom. THAT'S WHEN MY

LIFE CHANGED FOREVER!! Dun, Dun, Dun!!!!

So I rushed to my room, furious since my mother hadn't told me in advance, and began to pack as fast as possible. In a few minutes, I was done packing enough clothes for a month or two. I figured I could wash my clothes. Then, I ran to the kitchen and packed boxes of my favorite snacks. I looked at the clock and realized I had about five minutes. I did a quick check and made sure I packed everything.

I had less than 60 seconds to put on my shoes, run across the courtyard, get through the gate, say all my goodbyes, give hugs and kisses to loved ones, and get inside the Lamborghini. In an hour, I started traveling on a train.

In a couple of hours, we arrived in Miikay. It was so beautiful and yet not so familiar. I already missed home. I needn't tell you I missed my room and my mother shouting at me for doing naughty things.

I was so sad and busy day dreaming when a man came and told me we had arrived. Then he gave me a bag that said, "Genius School Supplies."

When I came out of the train, I saw a big

building. It said 'THE GRAND MIIKAY FINISHING SCHOOL' in big letters. I grabbed my school bag (the one the man was holding) and rushed out of the train.

Outside a lady greeted me. "Good morning princess," she said in a very stern voice. She bowed politely. I walked inside the school and looked around. The ceiling was like a big dome with a crystal chandelier and sky blue in color.

The floor was made of white marble and had a black rug. There were four beautiful staircases in every direction. I could definitely see that their entrance hall was a heck of a lot bigger than ours. There were two huge oak doors in front of me. Above them was a sign that said 'THE DINING HALL.' This place was so beautiful. I loved it so much. As I was looking around, I saw someone familiar.

Part 2

A Little Reunion

"Ava?" I said. She looked up. "Genius? Is that you?" she said. Ava Jeaning was one of my old friends from elementary school. "Hi," we both said. The lady who greeted me earlier said that we would be roommates and buddies for the school years here. We were both so excited.

Ava said she would show me the way to my room. We went up the north staircase, through a corridor, then down a staircase, and stopped in front of a huge tapestry with a lady in the front. "Each pair of roommates gets their own mini apartment thing. I don't know if all the others are guarded with tapestries. This is my first week at school.

The password for our room is 'Term and Time,'" Ava said. The tapestry swung forward. There was a short corridor with a door just ahead. Once we got there, I opened the door and saw a dimly lit room.

There were cozy armchairs and couches around a blazing fire. There was also a T.V. There were two staircases on either side of the room. Ava said the right staircase led to the bathrooms, bedrooms, and study rooms. The left staircase led to a small kitchen, dressing area, and a small dining table for two. She said we ate almost all our food in the dining hall. As I looked at the clock on the wall, I said, "When is dinner? I'm starving!" "Breakfast is at 8, lunch at 12, and dinner at 6. Oh, and I forgot, school starts at 8:30, and the lights are out at 10 PM.

We can still work but we must be in the drawing room by then. The whole campus is 50 floors! If you need it, the hospital wing is on the 7th floor. Tomorrow at breakfast, you'll get your schedule labeled with what floor your classes are on."

Ava looked at the clock. It was already 6. We both went out of the tapestry, down the corridor, and as we went up the staircase, Ava stopped. As I looked at why we stopped, I saw a boy. His hair was blond, and he looked the same age as me. My first crush at this new school! I was enchanted. I wanted to kiss him. Ava interrupted my thought and saw me mesmerized by his good looks. "That's Khan, by the way." She said all of a sudden. Still dazzled, I repeated, "Khannnn." Then I regained focus. I was frustrated with myself for inheriting a terrible trait from my mother; being so honest about my feelings. It's true, I'm a terrible liar.

Still blushing, I followed Ava to the entrance hall. I was wondering what the dining hall looked like. My question was answered as the doors opened. I greeted the headmistress, who turned out to be the lady who had greeted me earlier. It turns out her name is Lady Sycamore. Four oak tables were as long as one-third of a redwood tree. We took a seat at the first table in front of us. Many people were seated, which told me we were among the last people to get there. Khan was only a few seats away from me, which made me return to having butterflies in my stomach.

Lady Sycamore stood up to make a speech. "As you all know, we have many new students this year. I am your headmistress Lady Sycamore. You will spend 5-6 years at this finishing school. In December, you will have your winter break. The term starts tomorrow. You will get all your mail, letters, and schedules by bunny. All the dorms are in the corners and edges of the castle. Floors 15-20 in the main castle are off-limits. The hospital wing is on floor 7. The buildings outside the main castle are for specific classes only. On weekends, the students above 2nd year can go to Rainbow Rocks Village. You can take your free time to explore the rest of the Campus." Why do people keep on talking about the hospital wing? Do they think I'm going to need it or something?

"Now, the moment you've been waiting for: BEGIN THE FEAST!" Just like magic, food began to fill our plates. It was the most delicious feast followed by the most delicious ice cream dessert. That night, my stomach was satisfied and I slept well.

The most peculiar thing happened the next morning in the dining hall. We were enjoying yet another delicious meal, when all of a sudden, we heard a loud noise. Hundreds of bunnies came running in. They were carrying boxes and mail to deliver to each student. I opened my mail and inside was my schedule of classes.

First Day Schedule for Genius Green-Taylor

8:30 - 9:30 Numerals and Symbols
9:35 - 10:30 Quills and Parchment
10:35 - 10:45 Morning Break
10:50 - 11:50 Double Potions and Antidotes
12:00 - 12:30 Luncheon
12:35 - 1:30 Chemicals and Care
1:35 - 2:45 Ezalb Tryouts
2:50 - 3:50 Study of the Ancient and Old

It turns out Ava was wrong; it didn't identify the floors. But I figured it out. It was 8:20, so I headed for Numerals and Symbols. I didn't know anyone in class. Our teacher's name was Madam Ve. (vey). Our first lesson was The Romanian Num-air-ical Symbol Language.

We basically learned the roman numerals. We learned up to 30. I only remember up to 10! "Please copy all the things I say in your parchment book," said Madam Ve. She wrote all the symbols on the chalkboard. We copied them in the parchment book. "On the count of three please recite all the numbers we have learned," said

Madam Ve. "One, two, and three." For homework she told us to try to memorize the numerals.

I headed to Quills and Parchment next. I had Ava in my class, so I sat next to her. "Good morning!" said Professor Nor-Bell. "Please write an essay about how you like the new school," he said. I wrote about the feasts and the dorms. Those are my favorite things. I used six inches of parchment for my essay. We all turned in our essays at the same time. Then he taught us the one and only magic pledge. "For homework write 12 inches of your own magic pledge. Please hand them in next time," Professor Nor-Bell said.

Part 3

A Not-So-Friendly Encounter

I looked at my schedule and realized it was already time for the morning break. Ava and I rushed to our M.A. (mini apartment) We went to the mini fridge and decided to eat Vanilla Protein Cups. Vanilla Protein Cups are vanilla latte-flavored yogurt with protein powder. I headed for Potions and Antidotes next.

"You are late, Green-Taylor and Jeaning," said a cold voice. "Sorry, professor!" Ava said. "It is Professor Eld-I," he said in his cruel and cold voice. "Sit," Professor Eld-I commanded.

"Please take out your potion supplies and ingredients." We ended up sitting with Khan, whom I didn't see when we entered. He gave me goosebumps. "Today, we are learning about the shrinking potion," he said. He gave a small speech on the shrinking potion. He wrote directions and the ingredients on the board. "Please make the potion. You have ten minutes," he said.

It wasn't easy, so it is best not to explain everything. After making the potion, he wanted us to make antidotes. "You have 15 minutes. Go!" Professor Eld-I said.

Man, was this guy in a hurry. I poured the potion into my cauldron and added a few ingredients. I mixed, cut, fried, and simmered ingredients.

"Times up! Bring your antidote to me, now!" said Professor Eld-I. "I'll give you your grade next class." Ava and I left class together after turning in our antidotes. We made our way into the dining hall after class for luncheon. For lunch, we had chicken pot-pies, my favorite. Afterward, I had a mini chocolate croissant. Then I headed for my next class.

After all this time, it suddenly occurred to me that this was some sort of a "magic" school. Chemicals and Care were up next. This was all about our magic bodies and how to take care for them. Our teacher was Professor Yeisolf. (Yay, solf) This was the most boring class ever, so I'm never gonna tell you about it. I wouldn't say I like it. He wanted us to write a five-inch parchment essay on why we shouldn't use At- Naskik and what it does. It is some chemical that disintegrates your body.

All the first years headed to the Ezalb rink for tryouts for the next period. "I'm Coach Reab, and Ezalb is a popular sport in the sorcerer's world. It is a game where only some people have the talent to play." She tossed uniforms to each of us and told us to change in the locker rooms.

"Okay, we'll do one at a time. To play, you must play soccer in the air, but you stay up by breathing fire like a dragon. If you are successful, get in a line behind the blue cone. If you are not, go behind the red one", she said. A few people made it, and a lot of people didn't. Then came my turn. "Lean forward, open your mouth, take a big breath and blow!" Coach Reab said. I followed the instructions, and fire gushed from my mouth. I made the team! Khan also made the team.

Sadly, Ava did not. Our captain was in his 3rd year. His name was Shaylan. We had practice Wednesday, Friday, and Sunday.

Ava and I headed to Study of the Ancient and Old next. "Good afternoon, class; I'm Sir Teddy," said an old man with a gray beard. "We will learn about the founder and co-architect of this school. Her name was Alvina Baniya Cimonim. She was one of the most powerful enchantresses ever!" said Sir Teddy. He talked about a curse that was accidentally placed on her by a child. Though she was a great person, she was tortured to death by the curse. He went on forever. "Please give a presentation on her for Monday's class," said Sir Teddy.

By then, I was exhausted. It was four o'clock when Ava and I reached our M.A. We had Glorios. They are sugar cookies with a mint chocolate-flavored frosting. We had lemonade on the side. Then I started my homework. I did my Parchment and Quills homework first. We were supposed to write a Magic Pledge. I had to be careful since I wasn't doing a rough draft:

"Oh, Sorcerers and Sorceress's:
We shall stand together to make life work. We shall do everything with each other's permission, care, and love. If we experience failure, pain, or heartbreak, we will help each other through the hard times. We will live our dreams and finish the task that we were given. We should not kill, torture, or cause pain unless it were to save a life or for defense. We are here to show care and kindness. We will save each other and always be at each other's aid. The magic we use will be for purpose and assistance. We shall use spells for us and not against us."

After finishing one piece of homework, Ava and I went to dinner. We made our way to our table and squeezed in. Our cauldron glasses were filled with Italian Soda. I had never had it before, so it was delicious. We had a green salad with Italian dressing as our appetizer. After we finished the salad, our meal plates were filled with spaghetti and meatballs. I hadn't had this meal in so long. The food was delicious. My stomach was so full, so I waited five minutes before I ate dessert. Others didn't take a break and went straight for the Italian ice cream. It was so so so good.

After changing into my pj's, I decided to finish my homework since we had so much. I decided to do my homework for Chemicals and Care next since we had to write an essay:

"Have you ever heard of At-Naskik? This is extremely dangerous if you have any type of magic in your blood. Make sure you always check the ingredients in the products you buy. At-Naskik is a chemical that could kill you if you aren't careful. Some could say everybody magical has an allergic reaction to it. But how could everybody be allergic to the same thing? At-Naskik disintegrates you if you are magical in any way. Then it immediately begins to kill anyone you are related to. By following my advice, you should be able to be safe from At-Naskik."

Part 4

The Weekend

Writing about At-Naskik made me think about Alvina Baniya Cimonim so I decided to work on my presentation for Study of the Ancient and Old.

"Alvina Baniya Cimonim was born on October 1,1910. She grew up in a small town in Italy. She had 4 sisters and 5 brothers who were of all ages. Alvina was a middle child. She went to school for 8 total years in her entire life. She spent most of her time helping her mother do chores and taking care of the other children. When she grew up, after two years in college she became a teacher. Her eldest brother became an architect. Alvina and her eldest brother Luca decided to build a school. She became the co-architect and the founder of the school. One day a young wizard put a curse on Alvina. He did not know what he had done, until it was too late. The curse tortured Alvina to death, before she got married or had children of her own. She passed away May 18, 1940. It was later thought she died of At-Naskik because her brothers and sisters perished shortly thereafter, but the mystery remains."

I gave the presentation to Ava and she loved it! Thank goodness I was finally done with all my homework so Ava and I could enjoy the weekend exploring the campus.

The next morning, after breakfast, Ava and I explored the scenery. We went to see the amazing waterfalls on the campus. We saw the outdoor classroom for Mythical and Magical Creatures and we passed the entrance of Rainbow Rocks Village, a special place with restaurants, inns, and fancy hotels. As first years, we are not allowed to enter Rainbow Rocks Village.

Around noon, Ava and I got really hungry. We entered Flosiey's Village where we stopped at a pizza place for lunch. We both shared a cheese, olive, pepperoni, and pineapple pizza, and ordered frozen lemonade. Then we paid with Koobs. Koobs are sorcerer money.

Koobs are sticks that are used to pay for things. There are 1 cent, 2-dollar, 7-dollar, 17-dollar, 40-dollar, 150 dollars, and 1000-dollar sticks. Thank goodness Koobs are small. Each stick is a different size, which is how you identify them.

After lunch, Ava and I decided to go back to our M.A. We had finished doing our homework and editing each other's essays. Luckily, we didn't have much to do. We got pretty tired and decided to relax. We watched Enola Holmes, which ended right before dinner. At that time, we were both hungry and exhausted. For dinner, we had lamb curry with saffron rice. Then for dessert we had Turkish delight.

The next morning, we slept in. After our avocado toast breakfast, we decided to explore the building. Since we already saw outside, we explored inside:

Colorful chandeliers, diamond chandeliers, forbidden rooms, trap doors, classrooms, KHAN!!!!!!, more forbidden rooms, teacher's study, more trap doors, forbidden rooms, more forbidden rooms, even more forbidden rooms, even even several multiple forbidden rooms. I wonder what they keep in those rooms!

The next day was Monday. We went to class and turned in all of our homework. I don't think Professor Eld-I likes us much. On Mondays, we had that mythical creature's class. We worked with Aquafina-Fijis. They blow water at you if you don't treat them like royalty. Mr. Cera (Sarah) was our teacher. After class everyone was soaking wet. For homework, he gave us enchanted

Aquafina-Fijis. We had to practice treating them like royalty but they didn't squirt any water at us; just mist. Thank goodness.

After class, we saw Khan. He was coming toward us and his face was red. "Hi Genius, d-do you want to be friends?" he said. I didn't answer, I just stood there in shock. "Never mind, forget I even asked." And he ran off. "Wait! Khan! Come back! Of course, we can be friends," I said. "Really? You actually mean it?" he said. "Of course!" Ava left. Khan and I went to get a snack, yogurt parfaits.

Did he have a crush on me?!!!

The next day, I felt really sick. But we don't need the details. I skipped class and went to the hospital wing. Good thing I remembered where it was. I guess I did need it after all. It was huge and had lots of equipment. On my right, there was a sign above a doorway that said, 'STOMACH BUG.' I headed over there. "Oh, hello dear, come and have a seat over here," a lady said as she pointed to a chair. I sat down. In a few minutes she came over and introduced herself. "Hello dear, I am Mrs. Blanket. What seems to be the problem?" she asked. I told her I wasn't feeling well. She listened carefully and instructed me to do five jumping jacks while drinking apple cider. What's that going to do I thought. Is this lady Cuckoo Bananas or what? Like an involuntary movement, my body started doing what she commanded. BOOOM! I WAS BETTER!

I missed the first two classes and was late for the third. Professor Eld-I was really strict about it. "Sit down now!" He ordered. I got detention for three days! How does this guy not understand that people get sick? What is he, an invincible tyrant?

After the day was over, I headed for Eld-I's classroom. He made me write "I will not be late for Potions and Antidotes" with ink and a quill.

Part 5

Trapper

A few weeks had passed since my detentions. Little did I know, things were about to take a turn for the worse. Ava, Khan, and I were walking in a sus corridor when we spotted papers lying on the ground. We took a peek.

WELCOME TO THE WEDDING!

SHNAKE ELD-I +PLASTIC CUDDLES

The wedding of Shnake and Plastic, will take place on December 2nd of 2005. Be there at 8:24 sharp. Don't be late. In the woods."

"What are you idiots doing?" We heard someone say. "RAEB AMAMA!" A bright flash of pink light is all I saw. A portal opened in front of us and we fell in. Vaguely, we heard someone yell. It felt like we were falling into space, but for forever. We all hit the ground with a hard thud. A spell must have been cast on us. That was the only explanation for our whereabouts.

"Where the hell are we!?!" I heard Khan yell. "Ava, Khan, where are you guys?" I said. "Here!" He said. We ran towards each other. "Are you alright?" We said together. "Where's Ava?" I said. We heard a distant high-pitched scream coming from behind us. "Help! Run!" Was all I heard.

A giant beast was charging at us. It looked like a huge teddy bear, but with a clown nose and slits for eyes. "Grrrrrrrrr!" It sounded like nails on a chalkboard. Ava was running for her life.

There was blood dripping from her arm and she was clutching it. It looked like she broke it. "What the hell is that thing?" I said. Then, as I looked back, I tripped and fell. My friends tried to help me, but it was no use. It picked us up and tossed us into a cage.

"Genius. Genius. Wake up." Ava was shaking me awake. "What happened?" I said. "You don't remember?" she said. "No. What happened?" "We were chased, by a big teddy bear pennywise thing." Ava said. "That was real?" "Yeah, how do you think I broke my arm?" "I guess I must have got a concussion or something," I said. I looked at Khan. He also looked pretty banged up as well. "Oh, crap," I said. "This is all my fault. We shouldn't have read that stupid wedding invitation." "Genius, it's not your fault." Khan said.

"Guys, how are we going to get out of here?" Ava said. I got up. "Let's make a plan." "Sure, we can make a plan once you change." Khan said. I looked down. I was all wet. "Wait what, we're all wet!" I said. "It peed on us," Ava said. I guess Ava and Khan changed while I was unconscious.

"Action I'm vegan," I said. This was our signal. "Trapper", our teddy bear was asleep. Khan climbed out of the cell. Then he helped Ava and I. We landed with a thud. Trapper snored. Phew! We sneaked around a corner. Trapper almost peed on us again. Ava touched Trapper and she had an allergic reaction. It was Mealera. I had recognized this from something we learned in our Chemicals and Care class. She exploded and disappeared. Ava! We almost made it to the bed. We hoped that we could hide underneath for some protection. Trapper woke up and hit us with his tail. We flew on the bed and exploded. My mind suddenly went blank. The bed must have been another portal.

I woke up in the hospital wing. "Where are we?" I said. Ava and Khan were waiting for me. "Genius! You're awake. Let's go." They said. Was it all a dream? We hurried off. It was the end of the term. When we left it had been the middle. I guess time moved a lot slower where we were. Everyone seemed to have forgotten us.

We picked up our luggage which had already been mysteriously packed for us to leave school for winter break. Suddenly, there was an earthquake. The bright lights blinded me. We got sucked into a wormhole. As I was being pulled in against my will, I vaguely heard the words, "See ya later!" I felt like I was being stretched like chewing gum. I blacked out and that was the end. I felt like I died. Except, I don't really know what that feels like.

Not again! Suddenly, I couldn't think, talk, or hear. What happened? This couldn't be a dream.

Genius, Ava and Khan's adventures continue. Keep reading for a sneak preview.

BOOK TWO:

Genius and the Rumble of 1789

Genius The Sorceress

I was consumed by bright flashing lights. Then, all of a sudden it was utter darkness. I was so overwhelmed with what happened, I didn't have time to process anything. I, of course, didn't know where I was. I guess I could describe it as some sort of vortex or portal sucking me into another dimension.

I landed on the ground face first. My body was bruised in literally every place you could imagine. I'm pretty sure I got a minor concussion on the way down, because I couldn't remember anything. Everything slowly came back to focus. "Khan, Ava, where are you guys?" I said. "Here!" They both said. I could tell that it was coming from a distance. I tried to crawl over to their voices. I must've broken my leg, because it felt like it took 20 minutes to crawl 100 feet.

I looked around and saw everyone from the school unconscious. We sort of ended up near the beach. There were unicorns jumping over rainbows in front of me. They were white unicorns with horns about a foot long. They had rainbow-colored manes. The rainbows were in all the colors: baby blue, indigo, hot pink, turquoise, and purple. A boy who looked about twenty was riding one of the unicorns. He had dark blond hair, light skin and brown eyes. He was coming toward us.

"Hey, who are you guys and what are you doing in Realegealia?" he said.

Khan held up his hands, as if he were to be arrested. "We all come in peace," Khan said. "What's Realegealia?" I said.

"What do you mean, it's where you are right now. Wait a minute, how did you all get here?" He gestured to everyone else lying unconscious and scattered all over the beach.

"There was a huge earthquake back in Miikay. A portal opened up and sucked everybody inside. Then, it teleported us here." Ava said.

"Come with me right now!" the guy said. We followed him into Realegealia's main palace. This place was huge! It was the size of all Movie Magic put together. I've heard legends of sailors finding other countries and not returning. But no one believed them to be true. Would that be our fate?

DEDICATION

This book is dedicated to all the authors who gave me the ideas and inspiration to write a book. The book is also dedicated to my fourth-grade teacher, Mrs. Erbstoesser who helped me publish my very first book. My book is also dedicated to my parents who helped me create some funny puns. I would also like to thank them for their support and guidance.

Thank you!

ABOUT THE AUTHOR

Anaiya Shah is the author of Genius the Sorceress and many other books to come. Her very first book is the one you're holding right now. Anaiya is eleven years old and lives in California. She loves writing books and started writing them at a very young age. Anaiya has one brother who has big dreams of becoming an NBA player. Anaiya also enjoys acting and would like to become either an author, actress, or maybe even both. She plans on making the Genius series a ten-book series. You can see more of her at her YouTube channel, Naibunny2008.

www.ingramcontent.com/pod-product-compliance
Lightning Source LLC
Chambersburg PA
CBHW060647030426
42337CB00018B/3483